ABC's From Ghana,

With Love

By Betty Lewis Ellett

DEDICATION

To my family, with love

Bryan, Gina, Zeke, Pam, Greg, Webb & Christopher

ABC's from Ghana, With Love

by Betty Lewis Ellett

Photos by: Betty Lewis Ellett
And the members of the Ghana Delegation

Donna Hudgins, Tom Edwards, Milton McNatt,
Mary Raye Cox, Heather Howe, Betty Lewis Ellett

Published by
Dementi Milestone Publishing
Dementi@aol.com
www.dementimilestonepublishing.com

Betty Lewis Ellett, Author

ISBN: 978-0-9823348-9-8

Graphic Design by
Jayne E. Hushen
www.HushenDesign.com

To obtain a copy of this book contact Dementi Milestone Publishing
www.dementimilestonepublishing.com

or

Betty Lewis Ellett
beellett@aol.com

INTRODUCTION

Young boys and girls will enjoy reading and listening to "ABC's from Ghana, With Love". This book introduces the alphabet and the culture of Ghana in a creative, colorful, attention holding and interactive manner. Children will enjoy seeing the differences in what other children's homes look like, ways they dress, foods they eat and in the similarities found in love of books, reading and family.

Enjoy sharing this with children you love!!!

Happy Reading!!!

ABOUT THE AUTHOR

A first time author, Betty Lewis Ellett, has spent 30 years in the field of education. She has worked with students from preschool to community college level. It has been her joy to serve as family literacy specialist for a Head Start program for the past 18 years. In that capacity, she has helped establish a children's library, volunteer reader program and book give away program, giving away 17,000 books to date.

Through her involvement in her church she has traveled to Ghana, West Africa twice. She fell in love with both the country and its people. On the second trip she, along with members of the Ghana Delegation, were able to take a children's library to Osu North Presbyterian Church.

In addition, Betty is an artist and photographer.

"ABC's from Ghana, With Love" is an outgrowth of the above life experiences.

Betty enjoys art, photography, tennis, literacy work, reading and mission projects. The first 1,000 copies of this book will be given to Head Start children in the Fredericksburg area thanks to generous community donations.

Betty, a Richmond, VA native, lives in Fredericksburg, VA. She is the mother of one son and a newly treasured daughter-in-law.

ACKNOWLEDGEMENTS

The Presbyterian Church, Fredericksburg, Virginia

Osu North Presbyterian Church, Accra, Ghana W. Africa

Presbytery of the James, Richmond, Virginia

Ghana Delegation Members

Fredericksburg Regional Head Start

Dr. Marge Klayton Mi, University of Mary Washington

Sisters, Joy and Sally Abbey

Riverside Artist, Peg Larose and Carol Phifer

Gina Whitticar

Dear Friends and Family who have listened!!!

Deepest gratitude goes to the following donors whose funding allowed the first 1,000 copies
of this book to be given to Head Start, Virginia Preschool Initiative and Early Childhood
Special Education children in Virginia Planning District 16:

PNC Bank

Kohl's Department Store

Joe Wilson, Perma Treat

Carolyn Mathur

RLCC (Regional Literacy Coordinating Committee,
    Planning District 16)

Brenda Sauls & Lamoine Knefelkamp

Community Foundation of the Rappahannock
    River Region

Ronnie and Shirley Weade

Fredericksburg Kiwanis

Salvation Army, Women's Auxillary

Last, but far from least, thank you to Wayne Dementi for having faith in this project and being
a never ending "cheerleader" and to Jayne Hushen for doing amazing design work!!!

A... is for Aba House.

Aba House is a home in Ghana, West Africa. It was our home on a trip far away from our homes in the United States.

a

B... is for bread.

Bread is delivered to homes, sold in the streets and grocery stores in Ghana. Some ladies carry bread on their heads in containers. Just put butter on the bread and you are in for a treat.

b

C... is for caftan.

Many people in Ghana wear loose fitting clothes called caftans. They are made from bright, beautiful colored cloth. They keep people cool in the heat. Ester wears a pretty caftan while she works on the books in the children's library.

D... is for Dad.

This dad and his son are crossing the street. The dad is holding his son's hand. He wants to keep him safe. Do you look both ways when you cross the street? Does someone hold your hand?

d

E... is for eye glasses.

Our friend "Joy" wears eye glasses. Eye glasses make it easy for "Joy" to enjoy books. What a pretty girl! Do you wear eye glasses?

F... is for fish.

Fishermen are using fishing nets on their fishing boats to catch fish.
Are you fond of fish?

f

G... is for girl.

These girls in Ghana are wearing gorgeous dresses. They look good.

g

H...is for homes.

These beautiful homes are in Ghana. Houses look different in different parts of the world. Habitat is another word for home. Have you ever seen habitats that look like these?

h

I... is for island.

There are islands all over the world. This island is on Lake Volta in Ghana. Islands have water on all sides. Have you ever been on an island?

i

J... is for journey.

A journey is a trip. You can take a trip in a car, on a boat, in an airplane, walking with friends, on a jet ski, when you join friends on the school bus or when you read a book. You are taking a journey to Ghana today. Would you like to take a journey on this jet ski?

j

J

K... is for kente cloth.

"Eddie" is our weaver friend. He is a very kind kid. He shows us how he weaves kente cloth on his loom. Kente cloth is used in Ghana to make clothes for very special occasions, table cloths and many other things.

L... is for library.

Boys and girls in Ghana like to go to the library just like you do. Children in Ghana like to listen to stories and check out books to help them learn about new ideas and places.

1

M ...is for Mom.

This mother says good bye as her children go to school. Her baby is wrapped in fabric and is close to mommy. Does your Mom walk you to school or to the bus stop?

m

n ... is for necklace.

This girl is wearing a necklace made of beads. Her family has a business that makes beads and jewelry to sell. She looks nifty and nice wearing her necklace. Do you like to wear necklaces?

n

O...is for ocean.

The beautiful ocean is just outside this garden gate. We open our windows to see the ocean view.

P… is for plantains.

Plantains look like long, thin bananas. People in Ghana make plantain chips from them and carry them on their heads to sell. When you pop them in your mouth they taste like sweet potato chips.
They taste good!!

Q ...is for quiet.

It is quiet in the rain forest. You do not hear people's voices. When you walk on the bridges, at the top of the rain forest, you do not want to be quick. You want to go slowly and hear all the sounds the birds and animals make.

R... is for rain forest.

There is lots of rain in a rain forest. It makes trees and plants grow very tall. Scientists research the trees and plants to find cures for people who are sick. We need to protect the rain forest.

S... is for sisters.

Sally and Joy are sisters. Sometimes they have fun dressing alike. Do you have a sister? Do you like to dress like your sister?

S

T...is for thatch.

The roof on this home is made of thatch. Thatch can be made from straw or reeds. Have you ever seen a thatch roof? It keeps this family dry during the rain, shaded from the sun and safe just like the roof on your home does for you.

t

...is for umbrella.

This tree grows in Ghana. Why do you think it is called an umbrella tree? If you stand under the tree you can usually find shade from the hot sun.

V... is for vegetables.

Various vegetables are grown in Ghana. They are sold in stores and on the streets. Veggies are good for boys and girls in Ghana and everywhere. Do you like vegetables?

W... is for wood.

This man is gathering wood on his boat in Lake Volta. He will take it home to his family. They will use it to build fires. They will cook warm, wonderful meals.

W

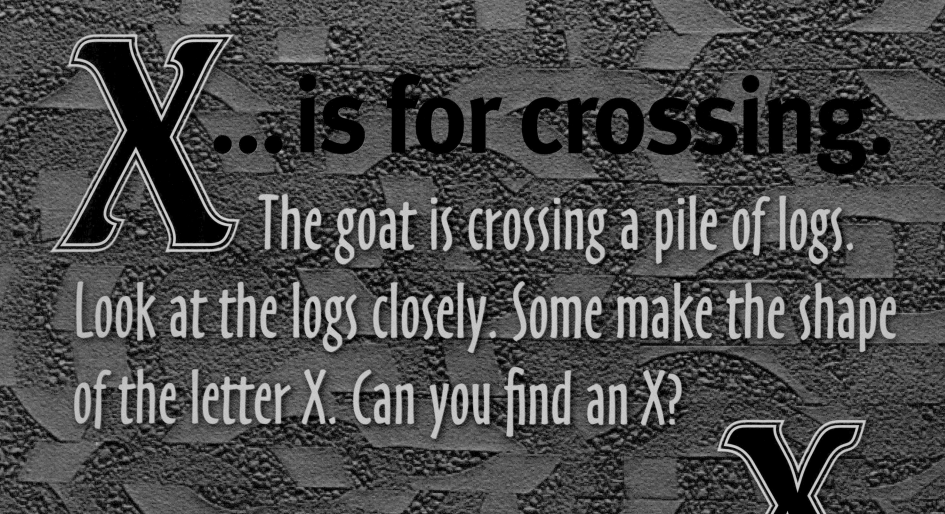

X... is for crossing.

The goat is crossing a pile of logs. Look at the logs closely. Some make the shape of the letter X. Can you find an X?

X

Y

...is for yams.

Yams are like sweet potatoes. In Ghana, yams grow all year long. These ladies are making yam balls. You might like yam balls. They taste yummy!!!

Y

... is for Zack.

This man's name is Zack. Zack zooms about the streets selling newspapers to people. Lots of people enjoy reading. Do you love to read and listen to stories?